WORSHIP SONGWRITINGTIPS

30 DAYS TO BETTER WRITING

DAVID J. PEDDE

WORSHIP SONGWRITING TIPS: 30 Days to Better Writing

ISBN: 978-0-99366-411-3

Cover art by josh@gomutiny.com

www.davidpedde.com

ACKNOWLEDGMENTS

Thank you to my Dad for the 1971 trip to the guitar shop in Barcelona, Spain that sparked my songwriting career.

Thank you to Mom for patiently enduring my earliest efforts.

Thank you to Debbie for keeping my heart song alive.

Thank you to my kids for making me a grateful dad.

Thank you to anyone who has ever listened or sung along with one of my songs.

Thank you to my students for faithfully and honestly writing what is on your hearts.

Thank you to those who will read this book and write songs for the Church to sing, giving musical voice to the pure worship of God.

Psalm 40:1-3

CONTENTS

ENDORSEMENTS

"David Pedde has written this refreshing and helpful book for worship songwriters. All songwriters will benefit. However, it is the worship leader that will benefit the most because he has written to their particular concerns, necessities, and subject. I heartily recommend this book to all those that give voice to our praises. If you're writing songs for the Church to sing, please read this book!"

~ Bob Kilpatrick, songwriter

"The first and only songwriting class I took was from Dave Pedde. I was a high school teacher who wrote songs in her living room, and I wasn't sure if they were good songs, or if it mattered. At that pivotal time in my life, Dave gave me a full range of tools that still inform my writing today. Dave has an amazing perspective on the integrated life and speaks seamlessly about the practical craft of songwriting, the heart of the writer, and the role of the faith-informed artist in a community. He is the kind of teacher and mentor I want the creative people in my life to know!"

~ Sara Groves, singer-songwriter

"I just finished your book. It has been the most important thing I have read on my sabbatical. It touched my heart so deeply that I could only read one or two tips a day the first few days because God was working in me so much. I love the format. I'm not in school, I don't want to read a thesis, and so many of the artistic books are formatted that way. I LOVE that you got right into the material in a simple, straightforward way. No word is wasted. No point is insignificant.

A simple and powerful read for beginners and veterans alike, reminding us that we don't create for our own pleasure, but for the worship of Our Heavenly Father and drawing His people to His side."

~ Kristi Northup, worship leader/songwriter

"Dave's songs are marked by easily singable melodies with thoughtful and biblical lyrics. I would consider him a scholar and theologian particularly in the field of worship. Dave's thirst for the Word and desire to represent Christ in his daily life act as an umbrella to all of what he does. In short, he lives out what he teaches."

~ Larry Bach, educator

FORWARD

I have had a few notable mentors in my life, one of them being the late Robert Webber. Bob and I, along with a couple of my graduate studies classmates, were enjoying a late-night bite together. I don't recall who asked first, but here was the question. "Bob, when did you start writing books?" Bob, then 70 years old with 40+ published books on the subject of Christian worship replied, "Sometime in my 40's." If my math is correct, that amounts to 1 - 2 books per year since then! He continued, "I didn't fancy myself an author, rather more of a scholar, teacher, lecturer. I wrote course syllabi, prepared lectures, journaled academically, and wrote position papers, but not books. Back then, several people encouraged me to simply *write down what I would say from behind a lectern,* so I purchased reams of foolscap, boxes of pens and set out to do just that."

I started writing worship songs a little north of 40 years ago. I've experienced the immense joy of hearing so many of those songs sung in worship, giving a musical voice to people's encounter with their Creator. I've "ghost co-written" 100's more worship songs and then enjoyed the privilege of tutoring aspiring songwriters in classes, seminars, and one-to-one mentoring sessions since the early 90's.

In the spirit of Bob Webber, I decided to write down some of the principles I have heard myself talk about over the years. The following worship songwriting tips are a brief compilation of those sayings.

Thanks for reading.

Thanks for writing.

Thanks for sharing what you write for the sake of His Kingdom.

Dave Pedde 2017

"

#1
read your bible daily (as in) let the bible read you daily

Worship is a relationship.

It is a relationship between God and His children, one that is initiated and sustained by Him.

He reveals Himself to us. He reveals us to us, and we respond in kind.

So, worship is an interactive conversational exchange.

Worship Songwriting is one way to give a voice to that conversation. It involves God talking with us and us talking with God. It then broadens out to include others, as we invite them to listen to Him and talk with Him accordingly.

Given these facts, it follows that the worship songwriter will be a student of God and His Word. And while we read the Bible, study it and memorize it with the goal of knowing and loving God better, we find that as we do so, it reads us!

Here is how this happens: The Holy Spirit comes and reveals Christ to us, guiding us into truth. This "grand reveal" not only speaks to His Character and deeds but also to the blunt truth about us, our character and deeds. As we focus our gaze on Him, we intimately participate in the graceful mystery of knowing and being known, loving and being loved. Incredible!

So, read your Bible. Get to know God and get to know yourself.

Make it an ongoing conversation.

Then write about Him and you and your interactions together.

Share what you write with others, inviting them into the story.

Lastly, I am often asked, "How can a person go about writing compelling worship songs?"

My response is always the same, "Read your Bible and then come back and see me."

"

#2
study the form of strong songs then form strong songs

Are you feeling stuck in your songwriting?

Straight ahead is my number one "getting unstuck" tip!

Every time I've taught songwriting over the years, I have quoted Grammy Award-winning songwriter, Jimmy Webb,

> "Lack of form...is the great failing with beginning songwriters. Either they aren't concerned with it, or they just don't understand it."[1]

By the way, Jimmy Webb is the only artist ever to have received Grammy Awards for music, lyrics, and orchestration, so it seems that he is a credible mentor on this subject.

In class, when we commence evaluating and working on songs, many students start out clearly unconcerned, even visibly disinterested, in any discussion of form. They assume that it will be boring, sterile, and will constrict their creativity. If I do succeed at coaxing them into an open-minded investigation of the subject, they find that increased understanding of form leads to greater freedom rather than less, their creativity being stimulated rather than stifled. It is so gratifying to watch eyes of understanding open and even better to see the results!

You may have heard of a decades-old study done with a group of young school children on the effect of fences/boundaries. The kids were ushered into a large playground with no fences to restrict their movements. They were instructed to play anywhere they wanted. Time-lapse photos showed them pretty much clustered together, remaining relatively close to the center of the field. Fences added, the kids were once again sent out to play. This time, apparently feeling more secure, they utilized the entire area. It turned out that some boundaries inspired rather than restricted exploration and creativity.[2]

So, study the form of great songs. Look into the overall design of intros, and verses, and choruses, and bridges, and endings. Then dig deeper into rhyme schemes, and phrasing, and numbers of measures in each section.

In the spirit of good form, build some "fences" for your songs and then go create!

"

#3
check your theology.
have others check your
theology. rewrite

Fellow Worship Songwriters and Leaders: What we do is super important.

The songs we write and lead are more than pop songs, more than catchy tunes, more than message bumpers, and more than openers or offering songs or closers. They are about God, and about us, and about our relationship with Him.

The best way to write about Him is to know Him…intimately.

Theology is the study of God. Initially, that may sound boring to the creative type. Study? Yikes, I thought this was about romance, and adventure, and art.

Let me frame it this way. Do you remember when you first were establishing a relationship with your significant other? You had serious interest in getting to know them and everything about them. They became known as your "love interest" for a good reason!

I've had an ongoing romance that began on a rare snowy Oregon evening in February of 1980. As she stood there shivering yet refusing the offer of my jacket, I knew this: I wanted to know everything about her! And I have been studying her ever since! I call it Debbie-ology.

Theology is the same kind of pursuit, only with the Lover of our Souls. When we sing about Him, inviting others to know Him, we had better be confident that we are calling them to a real relationship with the Real One! False God concepts abound in our minds and the church, let alone in our society. Notions about His Character falsely purported have done much to keep people away rather than drawing them home.

So, let's be theologians and befriend some. Let's know Him and make Him known in our lives and our songs.

#4
write often because writers write in the same way that teachers teach, dancers dance, painters paint, and plumbers plumb

Wow. Do I ever have to remind myself of this one over and over again!

I've gone through seasons of much writing and fluent creativity and then seemingly dried up for what I am embarrassed even to admit - years.

How about you? When do you write? When you feel

like it? When you're "inspired?" When there is the promise of a record deal or a pay cheque or some other kind of fame?

And then, what happens when you go years without anyone seeming to notice or care, all the while apparently noticing and caring about "that other" person's stuff?

Take a deep breath. Who are you? In other words, who has God called you to be?

How would you describe yourself? Better yet, how did you used to describe yourself before discouragement or anonymity or loss took over?

If you are hearing yourself say, "I am a songwriter," then start writing. Start writing again. Start writing regularly. Sing those songs. Share them.

Here's something I used to remind others in songwriting class:

> "Duty is neither an ineffective nor an irrelevant motivator."

A guy named Don Wyrtzen wrote a must-have book for worship songwriters called "A Musician Looks at the Psalms…"

WORSHIP SONGWRITING TIPS   david j. pedde

I love his reflections on the subject of inspiration:

> "We must not let the pressure of the modern life squeeze the song out of our lives. A sure way to let that happen is to sing only when we feel like it - when we're inspired. We must learn to sing in the night, when we're hurting, and when we're afraid."[1]

Once again. Are you a songwriter? Then, write songs.

Often.

#5
pray often, asking God what he would like others to know about him and then write that

Does it ever bother you when you are misunderstood, mistrusted or misrepresented? Do you cringe at that thought?

If you are like me, it upsets you to no end when your character is questioned or defamed, especially when it occurs through no fault of your own.

Have you ever been mischaracterized or falsely accused? If so, you know that it hurts.

Your thoughts echo something to this effect: "If they

only knew how terrific I am, how skilled I am, and what an asset I would be, they would hire me." "If they knew the real me, basing their opinions on facts instead of hearsay, they would take the time to meet me and get to know me." Or…"That's not me!" "I don't believe nor behave that way." "I am _____ (fill in the blank)!"

I am wondering how accurately our worship songs portray God. After all, we do sing about Him, about His nature, about His Character. When someone, especially that uninitiated someone, hears one of our worship songs, does it cause them to know God better? Does our portrayal of Him shatter any of their preconceived notions, particularly those that detain them at arm's length?   Or do they entice them to know the real Him?

If God is Who He says He is, then it figures that more people would want to know Him better, don't you think?

It might be helpful to take some time at this point to meditate on I John 4, especially studying verses 8 and 16.[1]

So precisely, who is He? What does He say about Himself? The fact that someone would resist God might well be due to single or repeated gross misrepresentations of Him in their minds. And those mischaracterizations might be perpetuated in well-intentioned, albeit misguided, song lyrics.

It remains an enormous responsibility for each of us first to know Him and then to make Him known.

Andy Park describes this primary pursuit in his terrific book for worship leaders.

The title? *To Know You More*.[2]

I'm with you, Andy.

As worship songwriters, let us not misunderstand, misrepresent nor mistrust God ourselves, passing on those "misses" to others by inaccurately characterizing Him in the worship songs that we compose.

Let us understand, trust, and represent Him in a way that adequately describes Him to those who hear our songs.

What does He want each person to know about Him?

Ask Him.

"

#6
write a "call to worship" song. an effective one does just that

As worship leaders, how many times have we heard ourselves say (or even shout over crescendoing pads and guitar riffs) something like this? "Good morning everyone. Welcome to our Church. Let's stand and sing and worship God…!"

Now, we do have great intentions. We are desirous that people genuinely connect with their Creator and each other. Is it possible, however, that we could maximize the effectiveness of this request?

Liturgically speaking, this invitation is known as "The Call To Worship."

In our modern "non-liturgy" (we do seek to be real and relevant after all…you know, not too "churchy" or "religious") we might be overlooking something more compelling than the call to standing and singing.

In everyday life, many different "calls" are almost universally understood and routinely utilized. A *call to order* gets a meeting started. A *call to action* motivates hearers to act, that is, to willfully participate in a worthwhile cause. (One of my personal favorites straight ahead!) A *call to dinner* heightens our anticipation of a delicious meal with family and friends. Who doesn't love that call?

Back to the Call to Worship.

An effective one not only signals the commencement of the service but also inspires the people to participative action while heightening their anticipation of time spent with family and friends in what we often refer to as "the Lord's house." And it is no coincidence that we routinely end up at His table, remembering His sacrifice as we renew our baptismal vows.

I describe it this way in *Worship First Principles: A brief look at the essentials for Christian Worship:*

> The CALL. We gather.
> This is the summons for God's people to join

in the communion of the Trinity. He welcomes. We respond. The goal is that each worshipper would experience a definite sense of the presence of the Living God, and would ready themselves for a full encounter/exchange with Him in community/ fellowship with other believers.[1]

In short, participants know where they are, why they are there, what they can expect and what is expected of them.

The Creator God bids us welcome and welcomed we are…home.

I dearly love the invitation God Himself gives to each of us:

> Come, all you who are thirsty, come to the waters; and you who have no money, come, buy and eat! Come, buy wine and milk without money and without cost. Listen, listen to me, and eat what is good…and you will delight in the richest of fare. Give ear and come to me; listen, that you may live. I will make an everlasting covenant with you, my faithful love promised…Seek the Lord while He may be found; call on Him while He is near.
> Isaiah 55:1-6 excerpts NIV

So, let's write some songs that cooperate in the setting of the table, that table where all are welcome to come and eat.

#7
read a psalm. put a few lines into modern language

The Psalms are inspirational on a number of levels.

They are real, and raw, and relational.

They tell of who God is, who we are, and how we can connect with Him in times of exuberant joy and deepest sorrow. A daily routine of reading and praying them has been a mainstay of God-relationship through the centuries, something worth considering by each of us living in this one.

Secondly, you may have heard the name Eugene Peterson, or perhaps know the name of his whole Bible paraphrase.

The Message was written for "two different types of people: those who hadn't read the Bible because it seemed too distant and irrelevant and those who had read the Bible so much that it had become 'old hat'…"[1]

The editors at biblegateway.com remind us that "language changes. New words are formed. Old words take on new meaning. There is a need in every generation to keep the language of the gospel message current, fresh, and understandable … to recapture the Word in the words we use today."[2]

Psalm 98 became the inspiration for Isaac Watts' "Joy To The World." Psalm 46 is paraphrased in Martin Luther's "A Mighty Fortress." Psalm 51 provided the impetus for "Make Me New"[3] (shameless plug of my song there).

So, read a Psalm in a few different versions, copy the lines most poignant to you personally, and arrange them into a singable lyric. Then try rewriting those same lines in your own words, using them to form the foundation of a worship song.

Have you ever found yourself complaining under your breath about stale or outdated sounding forms of music in the church? If so, consider the notion that songwriters like us are entrusted with the immense privilege and responsibility of breathing new musical life into timeless words!

In the paraphrased words of Isaac Watts' father (who incidentally was tired of hearing young Isaac complain about the music used in church), "Write something better."[4]

Let's take up the challenge, following the example set for us by the young man whose bio not so incidentally reads, "The Father of English Hymnody."

#8
start out in a new key for you … try another new key … explore

First off, a question: Are you a songwriter who typically "writes on" your instrument?

If so, here is something that might help spark brand new vistas of creativity for you.

Ok. So you know that thing you first play when you sit down with your instrument? I'm sure you can think of it.

Guitarist, it might be that big 'G' chord or that open power 'E.'

Keyboard player, it might be that favorite lick in 'C'

or 'F' or 'G.'

Next time you pick up (or sit down at) your instrument, deliberately avoid your usual thing and play something different, preferably in a rarely used (by you) key. You will immediately notice that the new key represents new tones, new colors, new timbres, new emotions and new ideas. It will be like starting out somewhere fresh or taking an alternate route to work or school. You'll notice previously unexplored scenes, experiencing the landscape from new camera angles.

A new key will also offer a fresh pallet for the song's tessitura (range of the vocal part).

Months after I had given this suggestion in a songwriting class, one of my students contacted me with some great news. He had been relatively stuck concerning songwriting creativity as well as in his guitar playing. He determined to become proficient in the key of B (5#'s) and set out to do so. A few months later he reported that it had opened a world of tones for him, sparking his songwriting creativity. The results were a wealth of newly composed songs along with a new favorite key.

Try it!

#9
ask yourself: "is this melody singable for the average person?"

One of the hallmarks of performing musicians is the ability to figure out what we do well and then to do it for others. It is called *being a professional*.

Our professional songs, then, are meant to showcase what we do well for others to listen to and enjoy.

When it comes to corporate worship, on the other hand, we need to look at what we are trying to accomplish in writing worship songs and leading worship.

While worship is not exclusively tied to music, worship music as a public expression is a group activity.

Group.

We do it together. We participate together. We sing together.

Together.

So, is it not incumbent upon the writers of this music to write music that can be sung together? This will have a marked effect on what we write and how we write. Agreed?

OK. The purpose of a worship song is not to highlight the range, skill or beauty of the worship leader's voice. Its purpose is to include and involve everyone in ways that are both meaningful and attainable.

What am I suggesting here? I think you know.

Some melodies simply have too many "tricks" for the average person incapable of the vocal gymnastics of the professional. Anything above C4 (guys) or C5 (ladies) is in most cases too high for the average person to sing. So what happens with all those exhilarating high notes (or octave flips) in songs written and recorded by worship artist tenors? People give up, stop singing, and listen instead of participating.

What about those delicious low notes sung by velvety voiced altos? Same thing.

We must remember that our job as worship leaders and worship songwriters is to give a song and a voice to the church (that is, the average folks).

So ask yourself when writing and recording your next worship chart-topper: Can the average person sing this?

Quick tessitura (vocal range) tip straight ahead: Most people possess a vocal range of a 6th to an octave. So keep it mostly between middle C4 to C5, and you should be good. By the way, louder songs allow for a little higher range.

Lastly, straighten out some of those crooked rhythms.

"Let the people sing."

(Note: If these thoughts are chafing you a bit, no problem, write for professional vocalists.)

"

#10
use a thesaurus. discover new ways of saying something. keep language fresh

A creative *(noun)* is a person who is creative *(adjective)*; one who creates *(verb)*. Makes sense.

Something that many, perhaps most creatives have in common, is their mild disdain for protocol as well as for any conventional helps in the creative process. They desire freedom, license and all things new and different.

If you can relate, may I suggest that even a creative person like you can use some creativity boosters at times? That is what the dictionary, and more specifically, the thesaurus, has become for me.

A lyricist loves words, and the dictionary is full of them!

Go ahead and consider the purchase of an enormous dictionary along with an accompanying thesaurus. You could also find good ones online. Familiarize yourself with both of them. As you do, vigorously resist the notion that this is mindless, dull, academic work.

Fall in love with words and learn bunches of new ones each week. An alternate word may contain a depth of meaning and shades of nuance that the one in your first draft may not possess.

And, as a bonus, you may just come up with a much sought after rhyme.

On another note, it is patently challenging to write a beautiful, memorable melody. With only seven pitches (give or take) in a scale to choose from, it's tough to remain uniquely original when composing one.

Regarding lyrical originality, however, it is curious to me how so many excellent melody writers often remark, "I'm not good with lyrics and most often find myself at a loss for words!"

Need encouragement? Read on.

There are approximately 170,000 words in the English language with the average person understanding and utilizing between 20,000 and 35,000 of them.

While there is admittedly a large percentage of those words that would never find their place in your worship song, there remains a whopping number that could.

For the sake of creativity, inventiveness, imagination, innovation, innovativeness, originality, individuality, artistry, inspiration, vision, enterprise, initiative, and resourcefulness (see what I did there? … smile), get yourself a thesaurus.

“

#11
guitarists, try writing without your guitar. keyboard players, try writing without your keyboard …

You may have read the title of this tip and thought to yourself, "No way! I have never done that and can't picture myself even trying."

The whole point of this tip is merely that of knocking you outside of your comfort zone.

You may not fancy yourself a singer at all and prefer to keep it that way. Frankly, you may not have been born with the voice of an angel. But you were, in all likelihood, born with a voice.

Your voice is unique to you, something that distinguishes you more than almost any other feature. It was the first thing that your parents heard as they anticipated your scream and will be the last thing that your loved ones remember as they huddle close, straining to make out your final words.

Nothing more intimately translates emotion than your own voice.

I didn't say that you need to be a professional singer or even that others need to be subjected to your voice if the tone is noticeably unpleasant (Heh, console yourself with the fact that you are gifted in other areas. Almost no one has it all!). But I am saying that you need to use it as God's unique gift to you by "letting it go" in worship to Him.

Many years ago, I was rehearsing a traveling group that represented the University where I taught. As we prepared to record, the students were presenting original songs for consideration. One of them, a skilled guitarist, had written several songs but always had another student sing them. When I asked to hear him sing one of his originals, he sheepishly replied, "I don't sing." "What do you mean, you don't sing?" I pressed, "How did you write this song if you don't sing?" He clarified, "Well, I sing, but only by myself, not for others." I gave it one more try. "Well, I'd like to hear you sing it. It is just us here."

When he finally relented and sang it for us a few weeks later, something magical happened right on the spot. His own voice singing his own song in his unique way accompanied by his feelings and experiences was undeniably captivating, springing the song to life for all of us. It was his. It was him. That terrifying beginning became the catalyst to a life-long singer-songwriter career.

I am not saying that fame and fortune lie ahead of you if you try singing.

I am saying that boundless creativity may be unlocked if you just put down your guitar or back away from your piano once in a while, and sing your heart out.

"

#12
read some great lyrics.
listen to those great
lyrics. in that order

A great song is great in every aspect: melody, harmony, rhythm and lyric.

Is there anyone out there guilty of attempting to hide a weak lyric behind a cool hook, or melodic guitar riff, or delicious beat? Can I get a collective "Ouch?"

I contend that a lyric must be great without the music backing it up. If it is, the music will serve to enhance the words, not outshine them. If it isn't, then it might be what has become known as putting "lipstick on a pig." Or as theologian Charles H. Spurgeon put it way back in 1887, "A hog in a silk waistcoat is still a hog."

Enough of hogs.

How did we all learn to play skillfully on our instruments? We watched other experts, and we emulated what we saw. We engaged in systematic practice, and we kept at it. The longer we played, the better we played.

Practice. Practice. Practice.

Simple.

I believe it is called something like "the law of sowing and reaping."

How then can we become great lyricists?

It's obvious.

Here's a quote that I have used over and over (and over) in songwriting classes.

> "All elements of the song (Melody, Harmony, Rhythm, Lyric) work together to enhance the feeling of the meaning of the song."

Desirous that my students get (and live) the point, I do my best to systematically drum it into their consciousness as a kind of songwriting mantra.

At the beginning of each class, I ask each person to rate their proficiency in the four areas: Melody, Harmony, Rhythm, and Lyric. Hands down, the element that perennially scores weakest is…drum roll please…you guessed it – LYRIC!

My admonition for the lyrically-challenged is always the same.

Read, read, read some great lyrics. Notice - not, listen, listen, listen to some lyrics.

Why?

It stands to reason that a piano player will be drawn to the piano part, the drummer to the rhythm, and the singer to the melody. While the melody does provide the musical vehicle for the lyric, they are not one in the same. It follows that the ear will be drawn to (even distracted by) whatever are the strengths of the listener, not the weaknesses.

When attempting improvement in lyric writing, my encouragement is to turn off the music, make a hot beverage of your choice, don personally calibrated spectacles, and read, read, read.

Oh yes, then, write, write, write. Simple.

#13
write a jingle or bumper for an upcoming sermon series

I think that we may have been trendsetters.

It was the mid-eighties. The notion of advertising a "sermon series" was not yet a thing. At the time, I was the music and worship pastor at London Gospel Temple in London, Ontario, Canada. During late May one year, our senior pastor Bob Smith announced an upcoming summer focus/sermon series to our pastoral staff.

Naturally, I began brainstorming service planning ideas including worship song selection and various creative elements including "special" music, dramatic elements and the look/feel of the sanctuary. I set out to have our sign painter design and paint a huge sign with the title of the series emboldened on it (novel stuff for way back then!): "MY BEST FRIEND."

The idea was for each service to feature one person from our congregation by having them share a brief prepared testimony describing how they met Jesus (their Best Friend). Pastor Smith would then follow up with a message designed to help people come to know Christ.

It has always been my contention that a church worship leader has "resident psalmist" responsibilities. That is - it is our job to give a unique voice to our individual congregation's unique worship. Rather than perpetually defaulting to so-called top worship hits from around the church world, we are charged with personally creating and facilitating others in fashioning worship expressions, be they songs or other forms.

So, I set out to do what I always do, write a song. I bantered around the "best friend idea," for several weeks, coming up with what I thought to be a most catchy tune.

Funny story: I do have a memory of working on the song one Sunday afternoon before our jazz band rehearsal. Our jovial bass player, who shall remain nameless, walked into the room and blurted, "What's that? That sounds a lot like the new milk commercial on the radio!" Undeterred by the dairy comment, I forged on, writing a song[1] that was to become not only a themed response song for that series but a staple of mine for years to follow.

Recently, I was in a conversation with a worship pastor who relayed that their senior pastor was extremely reluctant about using "homegrown" music in their church. I suggested that he look at the upcoming message titles, research the themes, write accordingly, and then let the pastor have a listen. I suspect that most senior pastors would relish the idea of original music created to support a message or message series, especially if it enhanced the overall worship experience for the congregation.

Give it a go.

"

#14
make it simple enough to be accessible, innovative enough to be remembered

Let's talk about you for a minute.

You are a deep thinker. You are serious. You take yourself seriously.

You have something to say, ample to give, volumes to contribute.

You have a point to make and a platform upon which to make it - your songs.

Now, if you are honest, you would rather hear

someone say, "Wow. That is deep!"

Not, "Yikes…not much there!"

You want to be known for what you say (content) and how you say it (craft). And you desire your artistic endeavors to be innovative while you're at it.

Innovative.

Let's talk about worship songs for a minute.

Effective worship songs are those carefully crafted for people we will call "average worshippers." They aren't solo singers or virtuoso musicians. They are ordinary folks. For this music to be useful for them, it must serve their needs. The job is not to impress them, wow them nor shock them. It is, instead, to serve them by providing a voice for their personal and corporate worship.

Worship music must then be, by nature, accessible.

"Great," you're thinking, "there goes innovation! Out with innovation and in with accessible."

Accessible.

Accessible and Innovative.

Seems like the consummate oxymoron.

Let's talk about hits for a minute.

All great hits, as innovative and fresh as they may be, are accessible. Think about it.

At the symphony or the opera, no one typically sings along with the orchestra. Doing so might lead to one's early ushered exit.

At a pop (remember that "pop" is short for popular) concert, everyone sings along even at the risk of severely annoying the person next to them. Also - they are not shy at all about letting you know, yelling in your ear, "This is my favorite song!"

A hit becomes a hit because the average person wants to sing along with it over and over again. In short, this is because it is easy enough to be accessible to them.

"So, we are supposed to carelessly craft boring, run of the mill, industry swill with droning chords, and lifeless, stepwise melodies?"

No. We are going to craft hits.

Accessible. Innovative. Balanced. Hits.

Worship song craft mandates to keep in mind:

. Accessible to the average person, but catchy.

. Singable for the average person yet interestingly innovative for the musician.

Lastly, remember the hymn-writing, theology-expounding, thesis-on-the-door nailing, 16th century German named Martin Luther? It is reported that he effectively married accessible bar tunes to meaningful Psalm lyrics and created a hit...or fifty.

You can do it.

"

#15
edit out as many filler words as possible. they are not needed. no, they are not. no. no. no. no …

Have you ever taken a public speaking course? If so, you may remember tutoring on the strict avoidance of filler words. They are those verbal fillers employed particularly in public speaking in an attempt to bridge silent moments between connecting thoughts.

All too familiar culprits include "Uh," "Um," "Like," "I mean," "Hmm," and "So." Also included on the naughty list is my personal favorite, "You know." That one gets me every time, you know. (Wink)

Filler words clutter up the sonic space and draw

undue attention to themselves. Their most significant crime is that of diluting the thesis by watering down the primary points. The average listener unconsciously bales out on the speaker with important communication getting lost.

To the business of songwriting.

As you know, a lyric exists in time. The beat of the music propels the lyric forward. Face it - there is no time to waste on nonessential words in those precious 3 to 4 minutes.

In songwriting, "Uhs" and "Ums" and "Likes" are likely not the problem, however…

The overuse of conjunctions, prepositions, and pronouns might be.

Here's an idea:

Step One: Write your lines freely and unedited.

Step Two: Read over and highlight essential nouns and verbs.

Step Three: Look over again and cross out all conjunctions, prepositions, and pronouns.

. Conjunction examples:

and, because, but, for, if, or, when
. Preposition examples:
after, in, to, on, with
. Pronoun examples:
I, me, mine, you, yours, his, her, hers, we,
they, them

Step Four: Cautiously insert back in whatever conjunctions, prepositions, and pronouns are critically necessary to preserve meaning.

Step Five: Do it again.

Um, like kinda try it and you know it might help... you know.

"

#16
place strong words on
strong beats

The following are the syllables and single syllable words found exclusively on the downbeats of each measure in a timeless 16 measure gospel song:

> "maz," grace, sweet, sound, saved, wretch, me, once, lost, now, found, blind, now, see.

What classic song is playing in your head right now?

As you know, *Amazing Grace* was written in 3/4 time.

Yes, that's the old familiar "Oom-pah-pah."

And you would also know that there is only one strong beat in 3/4 time - beat one, the downbeat.

Let's review strong beats and weak beats in the meters which you are most likely using these days:

$\frac{4}{4}$ (1 2 3 4)   Strong downbeat, secondary beat

$\frac{3}{4}$ (1 2 3)   Strong downbeat

$\frac{6}{8}$ (1 2 3 4 5 6)   Strong downbeat, secondary beat

Think of it this way.

When presenting a speech, one highlights the significant headlines on their outline.

Next, they spotlight those same points in the media presentation using different colors or bolded fonts. They do this to ensure that the audience not only hears but receives the important message they are attempting to convey. Because full understanding of that message is vital to them, they avoid any clutter that distracts from it. In addition to the visuals, an accomplished speaker also uses inflection (tone and volume) in their voice to draw attention to the central themes.

Similarly, when writing and presenting a song, the songwriter desires to draw primary attention to the central message by highlighting the points that support it while avoiding any distracting clutter along the way.

The optimum way to do that is to situate important words in conspicuous places. Those places are the strong beats. Strong beats in music bring emphasis in the same way that bold colored fonts and heightened voice inflection do in public speaking.

Like any of the other tips I am offering, this one might come entirely naturally to you. Or you may have a lot of work to do.

Either way. Take out your lyric sheet. Highlight the words vital to the message.

Next, take notice of where you have placed them in each phrase.

Once you have ensured that they are on strong beats, think about how you are going to arrange the song musically to highlight your message. For example - avoid having a drum fill (or other musical clutter) playing over top your most important words.

(Oh wait. That's another subject…or another book).

#17
write and record one
new hook per day

I had to include at least a few tips that had the air of impossibility attached.

Seriously - who among us with our jam-packed North American rush-here, rush-there lives could ever hope to accomplish something like that? Writing every day? Recording every day? In my dreams. Might as well quit before I start.

Sometimes we fail to start for the pure fear of not following through. Everyone knows what it's like to start the new year off with a bang and a fist full of resolutions, only to fail within a few weeks, give up and quit. A few false starts and we quit for good.

Enough negative talk. Let's remove the excuses and

go for it!

It was Antoine de Saint-Exupéry who famously coined, "a goal without a plan is just a wish,"[1] so let's get started. We have songwriting goals so let's regroup and make a plan.

Part One: Write one new hook per day. Let's conquer this one.

I didn't suggest writing a complete song every day, but instead, one new hook.

Songwriters think in hooks. We have an internal intuitive response to the world around us - music. It plays in our heads, even keeping us awake at night. It is how we process and how we communicate.

So make a plan to write one down…every day. Keep a journal somewhere. In a notebook. On a smartphone. On paper. In Evernote. Somewhere.

Part Two: Record one new hook per day.

I didn't suggest building a recording studio in your spare room, although that would be a dream.

We all know the joy of a catchy tune, a sweet groove, an innovative riff, or a memorable lyric dancing around in our head. We have a front row seat to the concert, and it is exhilarating!

But we all know the panic and acute sense of loss when we simply cannot remember it later.

We need to capture it somehow!

Of course, you can write down the lyrical hook in a notebook, but unless you are sufficiently skilled in musical notation, you might lose the tune from your memory altogether.

Hopefully, excuse number two started to fade when you remembered that you own a smartphone or some other great gadget that has a record button on it!

Commit to this tip. Put it on your calendar. Try it for a month.

You may well find that a habit has formed and you'll be on your way to accomplishing what you set out to do - writing, capturing and sharing beautiful songs with the world.

#18
remember that you don't have to write a pre-chorus for every song ... seriously, remember that

Church history is long so subsequently church music history is long. The scope of this book is not broad enough to include much on the subject.

Suffice it to say: 21st Century Worship Songwriting is primarily pop (popular) songwriting. A working knowledge of popular song forms is necessary when writing this music.

Here are a few 20th/21st Century forms.
- . Simple Chorus Form
- . Verse-Chorus Form

. Verse-Chorus-Bridge Form
. Twelve Bar Blues Form

The Verse-Chorus and Verse-Chorus-Bridge Forms have by far been the most utilized since at least the 1950's.

So, where does the section that has been come to be labeled the Pre-Chorus fit?

The 2000's and beyond may end up tagged as the Verse-Pre-Chorus-Chorus-Bridge (with multiple variations thereof) generation of worship music. I'm not convinced that this is necessarily a good thing - more on that in a minute.

Brief notes on Song Sections:

. Verse - generally sets up and supports main thematic idea.

. Chorus - contains both the song's title and central message. It often repeats at the end of the song.

. Bridge - can be an interlude after verse before the final chorus. It can also serve as an instrumental break. Sheila Davis describes it this way:
"Traditionally, the bridge takes the listener to a

new musical place, which sounds inevitable both in its arrival and its return to the final A."[1]

Now for the star of the show (or at least this tip). Drumroll, please…

> . Pre-Chorus - an optional (keyword: optional) two to four line section positioned immediately preceding every chorus in the song intended to propel the listener lyrically and melodically into the Chorus.

If the title of this tip has left you thinking that I am on an anti-pre-chorus crusade, you may rest assured that I am not.

I am, however, advocating for a couple of things.

First: Recognizing that increased numbers of sections translate to more complexity, make doubly sure that each section is strong on its own merit. It needs to contribute rather than clutter.

Second: As it does seem that virtually every current worship song follows substantially the same form (and chord changes - another subject … smile), try to make use of various forms for the sake of variety and innovation. Study each section and ask if it, back to Sheila Davis' words, "sounds inevitable."[2]

It is a must-have if indeed it is a must-have.

"

#19
try avoiding the words "i" and "me" and see what happens

For any thoughtfully honest observer of current worship music, it would be hard to argue against the fact that the trend has been towards 'me-ism' in the music. Other than the fact that we, as people, are increasingly affected by the cumulative cares of this world, I think that this has happened for a reason.

Question: Who writes these songs?

Obvious answer: We do.

Follow-up question: And who are we?

Answer: We are emotive creatures, in touch with our

inner feelings, also attune to the plight of the folks around us and of our world. We feel deeply and communicate transparently. Simply, we are artists, good at art, skilled in storytelling.

So, here is how it goes for me: Something touches my emotions. I ruminate on it, keenly mining my thoughts and feelings on the subject. Next, I sit down in front of a piano or take guitar in hand, then proceed to express those thoughts, feelings, and honest reflections.

As I do so, it is almost impossible to avoid the words "I," and "me," and "my."

The result is that many (dare I say most?) of our worship songs start out with an overt "me-focus."

Bob Webber was the most prolific author on the subject of Christian (particularly Evangelical) worship in the 20th century. He labeled this *narcissistic worship*, that is, "worship that arises from me….not a focus on God, not a focus on what God has done or what God is doing, but rather a focus on me."[1]

On worship and spirituality, he wrote:

> "Worship has become narcissistic, focusing on *me* and *my* praise of God; and spirituality has turned toward a preoccupation with *my* journey

of faith and *my* spiritual condition and experience…When we become narcissistic, the place of worship and spirituality in God's narrative is lost, and worship and spirituality become subject to the whims of culture."[2]

I am not suggesting that you put your feelings on the shelf. Your emotions, after all, are a large part of what distinguish you as an evocative artist.

I am suggesting that you shift your intentional focus to God's narrative, His story, find your place there, and write about Him first.

#20
use one main idea in each song. one.

Here's a simple question I sometimes ask the songwriter even before hearing their song.

"What is the song about?"

The response often goes like this.

"It's kind of hard to explain." (Red flag #1)

"It's about 'this,' and it's kind of about 'that.' (Red flag #2)

It also contains 'this thing,' and touches on 'that thing.'" (Red flag parade)

I realize at this point that I am going to have to

commit a lot of brain power to stick with the story. If I ever verbalize anything to that effect, they look at me like I've stolen their bowl of ice cream or spoken adversely about their puppy.

In reality, my intention is not to stymie their creativity, but rather to open their eyes to new possibilities.

"What if you have enough material for two songs or three? Wouldn't that be terrible (wink)?"

I think it may have been effectiveness guru Stephen Covey who said: "The main thing is to keep the main thing the main thing."[1]

Let's apply this to lyric writing. What is the main thing you are trying to say in this song?

Say it, then say it again, and again.

Find another main thing.

Write another song.

Repeat.

Voilà - you are a prolific songwriter!

#21
put a prayer to music - yours or someone else's

Often I sing my prayers. Not because I am a singer, but because singing seems to take heightened resolve for me, particularly if I am in a tough season in my life. I have often described my devotional life of prayer as messy.

Here is something I wrote in the Forward to my *Prayer Primer* book a few years ago:

> Depending on my immediate circumstances I have found my prayers ranging from the neatly academic to the desperately messy. They have been ordered, structured, and timed. They have been bombastic, scattered, even pathetic. Still, I pray. I pray because I want to know God. He is my Home.[1]

Daily recognizing His grace required for me to align my will with His, I attempt to follow the example of Jesus Who Himself cried in the garden, "Not my will but yours."[2]

A daily prayer song for me goes like this:

> Come now, Your Kingdom
> Be done, Your will
> And by Your mercies, please come and fill me
> 'Til the kingdoms of my heart bow to the Kingdom of the Christ
> Your Kingdom come, Your will be done.[3]

That's my prayer. That's my song.

What's yours?

Pause.

Additionally, there are a wealth of the prayers of others to explore. I do understand that evangelicals are not big on reading prayers, preferring the personally spontaneous over the carefully crafted.

But, could I encourage you to read some of the prayers of Jeanne Guyon or Archbishop Fenelon or Michael Molinos or Brother Lawrence? Perhaps read those of Henri Nouwen or Martin Luther King Jr. or

Mother Theresa or Billy Graham…to name a few.

To my knowledge, none of those mentioned above put their own passionate prayers to music. You could give them melody. Just an idea.

Over the years, hymn writers and composers of worship music have set prayers to music. It was in 1935 that American pianist, organist, composer, and educator Albert Hay Malotte set perhaps the most famous prayer of all time to music, gifting it to generations of worshippers to come. His "Lord's Prayer" is sung by Christians worldwide.

Join me in acknowledging him, "Thanks, Albert."

And we will thank you when you follow suit.

#22
write freely at first then edit using chord substitutions for variety

No matter the discipline, most of us desire to improve. I would like to think that my current songwriting is more refined, more creative, and flat out better than it used to be. Like you, I desire my songs to be fresh, sound somewhat current, and find their way into worship gatherings and people's playlists.

In all art, worship songwriting included, there exists a delicate dance between convention and innovation, old and new, familiar and unfamiliar, unity and variety.

It is imperative that unity and variety are both in play.

Unity serves to bring the whole together, legitimizing credibility to the listener.

Variety serves to spark interest, enticing the listener with a keen sense of adventure.

Both are needed.

Here are two questions I ask myself when I write a new song:

. What is there about this song that makes it sound familiar, accessible, comfortable, and stable?

. What is there about this song that makes it sound fresh, challenging, inviting, and adventurous?

I try to keep the unity/variety tightrope in mind realizing that leaning too far towards unity results in overfamiliarity (boredom) for the listener, and leaning too far towards variety leads to confusion (rejection) for that same listener.

On to chords for a minute. Proceed with caution.

If all of the above is swirling around in my head too early, my creativity is often thwarted by the phenomenon some might call "analysis paralysis." To avoid this, I try to write whatever comes out freely.

After mining my thoughts and emotions, then jotting down melodic lines and chords, I let it sit for awhile.

Next, I get to work on the theory side, reworking and substituting chords that add interest (variety) without distracting from the original intention (unity).

It is a delicate dance known as art.

Lastly, I always challenge songwriting students to bone up on their music theory knowledge, while at that same time reminding them that "the problem with music theory is that it is oh so theoretical!"

Avoid this by not only studying diligently but also putting theory into practice.

Write freely. Edit voraciously.

Create art.

"

#23
figure out the best tempo for the song. write it down and start there next writing session.

Anyone who has ever worked on music with me knows that I am a stickler for tempo.

A stickler. Guilty. True. I am super opinionated and picky on this.

To me, a bad tempo ruins a song more quickly than just about any other variable.

Too fast - deep groove lost, lyric rushed.

Too slow - energy drained, lyrical momentum stalled.

2 to 4 b.p.m. (beats per minute) up or down has the potential to make a marked difference.

So, who should be in charge of the tempo? The band? The drummer?

No!

You - the songwriter.

Buy a metronome, or download an app.

Learn how to use it, then turn it off.

Write your song. Express yourself freely, doing what comes naturally.

Near the end of the session, determine the point when it is feeling rhythmically pleasing to you.

Next, turn on the metronome to see where you are tempo-wise and make a note of it.

Next time you sit down to work on the song, set the metronome to your recorded tempo, turn it on, then sing and play the song.

Note how it feels now.

Too fast? Adjust.

Too slow? Adjust.

Make a note of the revised tempo then repeat this process until you love it.

Share the finished song with the band making sure to communicate the tempo to them.

Be a stickler for that tempo. A stickler.

It will pay off.

"

#24

have people read your lyrics then come up with thesis statements for the song. compare with what you were trying to say.

Any misunderstood person knows the frustration and accompanying pain associated with it.

Clear communication is fraught with difficulties for one reason. It takes two…the sender and the recipient.

The sender sends information while the recipient receives and decodes that information, responding according to what they have understood the message

WORSHIP SONGWRITING TIPS   david j. pedde

to be.

The primary objective of all communication is for the recipient to understand the intended message conveyed by the sender fully.

Play the *whisper game,* and you'll find out how this works…or doesn't.

Famed Irish writer George Bernard Shaw put it this way,

> "The single biggest problem in communication is the illusion that it has taken place."[1]

This illusion has the potential to frustrate both the sender and the recipient!

Anyone who has ever written an academic paper is familiar with the concept of a thesis statement.

A thesis statement, in essence, is a sentence encapsulating a particular premise. A possible vernacular description could be "here's what I'm trying to say here!"

It sums up a premise that proceeds to find support in the subsequent points.

You are the songwriter, the sender, the one who has a good grasp on what you are attempting to say.

Before unleashing your song on the world, have a few (or even more) recipients listen, "decode" and respond.   Ask them, "What is this lyric saying to you?" "Put the meaning behind this song into a sentence for me."

Compare it with the thoughts and feelings that coursed through you en route to their thoughts and feelings via your song.

Did you say it? Did they get it?

Do you need to try again?

#25
write songs for your personal prayer times. sing alone for weeks … months …years then share them

I wrote a simple worship song sometime in the 2000's with this title: I Believe.[1]

If you are a connoisseur of worship music at all, it doesn't take much effort to imagine what it's about or Who it's about.

The title and its understanding come naturally.

The song references our affirmative belief in God the

Father, Son, and Holy Spirit. It is a Creed, a statement of faith, an anthem describing Who God is and voices our response to Him.

Pause.

I need to tell you that I initially wrote the song for an entirely different reason. I didn't compose it as a "raw, raw, Go, God, Yes You are, Yes You are!" type of tune as a guy full of faith and positive vibes…

In truth, I wrote it at a time when I was struggling to believe, trying to believe, hoping to believe, desperate to believe.

Have you found that life's circumstances have a way of knocking naive, fairy-tale belief right out of you? You may have grown up "believing," then watched with dismay or even disdain while your so-called "faith" either slowly or abruptly faded.

Life happened. Your fragile belief system was challenged, and it failed the test.

I initially "wrote" my song *I Believe* at 3:00 AM while kneeling at the bedside of a child who simply would not recover.

I then whispered it in the hospital hallway pacing as my beautiful wife underwent two invasive brain cancer surgeries.

Over these many years, I've sung it again and again whenever I didn't know what else to do or to say.

Anyone who knows me knows that I love to pray. My favorite prayer in the Bible is this:

> "Lord, I believe. Help my unbelief."[2]

This was the prayer of a man whose son had an incurable disease. This father was despondent. He was admitting, possibly even screaming, "I am desperate. This is impossible. I don't have the strength, nor the will to believe. If You don't help me, help him, help us, we are sunk!"

My experience is that it is easy to sing "I believe" when life is sailing along. It's excruciatingly difficult to sing those same words when the ship is wrecked.

I tell young worship leaders and songwriters all the time:

> If your sad song doesn't make you cry, don't sing it.

> If your happy tune doesn't lift you personally with inexplicable joy, don't share it.

If you've never stared at God in wonder, speechless in His holy presence, don't open your mouth to explain Him to others.

Finally, if you've never doubted, don't peddle your untested "faith." It might not be real.

But if you have, then sing.

Let us hear you.

Let us join you.

Sing it.

#26
write a song for kid's worship. write another one.

Anyone sensing the call to France as a missionary understands job one to be that of learning to *parle Français*. Simply, effective communication requires a depth of understanding, not only of language but also of culture.

Anyone who has learned a new language also values the essential ability to think in that language as opposed to merely translating. To do so, one immerses themselves in the new culture and takes it on as their own.

Anyone learning a new language makes an additional discovery: The process of learning the "new one" has enhanced one's understanding of the "old one." Vocabulary, grammar, sentence structure, and related parts of speech all come alive. Remember high school English class?

As worship songwriters, our job is to give musical voice to worshippers, to write songs they can sing as worship expressions to God in their own unique language.

To write effectively for them, we need to learn, know, think, and write in their dialect, embracing their vocabulary as our own.

Teaching Songwriting II at North Central University was an exciting challenge for me. The class was not designed for beginners, nor the thin-skinned.

We would begin with an evaluation stage where each songwriter's obvious strengths and glaring weaknesses were identified through personal, peer, and professor evaluations. The class members would then design the semester's assignments for each other and off they would go. As you can imagine, the assignments were remarkably diverse, designed to present maximum learning challenge for each student.

One student received this assignment from his peers: Write six Children's songs for use in Kids Worship.

I am not sure that this particular guy had any interest at the time in children, let alone the desire to write for them. But something interesting happened as he set out to complete his assignment over the next two months. (The rest of the story is that he wrote fantastic kids songs, keeping it up long after class).

If you were to take up the same challenge, here are some outcomes you could expect.

You would learn:

. To make sure your theology is on point
. To write catchy hooks
. To create singable melodies
. To have some fun
. To write simply and directly
. To not take yourself so seriously
. That kids are awesome
. That kid's worship is a little less cluttered than that of those sophisticated adults you've been attempting to write songs for.

Give it a go.

"

#27
ask yourself "does this song pass the whistle test?"

During a quick lunch break one day during my final undergrad year in 1985, I was thinking about the fact that I wanted Christ to be fully seen in my life. I jotted down a few lines then grabbed my old Framus (yes - Framus) guitar, giving the lyrics a simple melody.

Ten minutes later I went to choir class (I was the student conductor) and taught my newly composed *Lord Be Glorified (In the Life of Your Servant)*[1] as a vocal warm-up. That sixteen measure chorus caught on quickly with my classmates, found its way into our repertoire, and was frequently sing in chapel services that year.

For decades afterward, I would receive thank you notes from people around the world explaining how that little song had given voice to their worship. Amazing!

Sometime in the 90's, I heard from world-renowned worship leader Bob Kilpatrick. Bob's eight measure song Lord, Be Glorified[2] had been recorded, re-recorded, and sung by millions of worshippers the world over, remaining on the CCLI top 100 list for 30+ years.

Bob, who called my song "The other Lord, Be Glorified" said that the secret ingredient in hit songs is that they can pass, what he calls, "the whistle test." You know, a melody that a person finds themselves whistling, humming or singing in the shower. It gets in their head, sticks in their ear, and comes out of their mouth at random times when they are not even consciously thinking about it. For that person, that song is a hit!

Some elements of a hit could be described as:

. Strong Title
. Inviting Hook
. Appropriate/Interesting Harmonies
. Appropriate/Interesting Form

Possibly the highest on the hit priority list would be a Catchy/Memorable Melody, one that passes "the whistle test!"

Somewhat of a worship songwriters dream come has happened to me on more than one occasion. For me, it tops having my song recorded, sung during a worship service, or viewed on YouTube.

Here it is:

Walking down a hallway behind someone who doesn't know I'm there, listening in while they sing, hum, or whistle a song that I wrote.

For them, my simple song has passed the whistle test, made its journey into their heart, and enhanced their worship.

(Insert sound of yourself whistling your favorite song).

#28
speak (don't sing) your lyrics, then ask if they flow well rhythmically

There is something equally important to meaning, word choice, and rhyme schemes in lyric writing.

Here it is:

Lyrical Rhythm.

Even in everyday speech, words flow not only pitch-wise but also rhythmically in a series of accented and non-accented syllables. We have a label for the speaker who shies away from these subtle nuances:

Monotone.

Naturally, we want to avoid this label at all costs when writing lyric, so how can we ensure that we do?

Teaching on this concept, I introduce something I call "Tum-tas."

Here's how they work:

> "Tums" are strong, emphasized syllables.
> "Tas" are weak, de-emphasized ones.

I have each person Tum-ta their own name, introducing themselves as such.

For example, my name is Tum ta Tum ta (Da-vid Ped-de).

What's yours?

Next. Try saying your name with reverse Tum-tas and notice how weird that sounds!

I then write several phrases on a whiteboard and have the students do the Tum-ta exercise.

Hea-ven-ly hosts will sing, will sing. Hea-ven-ly hosts will sing.

Tum-ta-ta Tum, ta Tum, ta Tum. Tum-ta-ta Tum, ta Tum.

Hear it?

Remember that these strong words (all of the "Tums") should land on strong beats.

Here is an exercise to try them out:

. ®Apple users employ ®Garageband. Others snap your fingers or find a drummer (Wink!)

. Set up a simple drum groove with the tempo and feel of your song.

. Speak (OK - Rap!) your lyric to the groove.

. Ask - how does it feel? If it feels great, then great!

. If it feels weird, then adjust the rhythms in order to put the Tums on the strong beats.

Try it.

Tum ta.

#29
learn some new chords and implement them

I played a lot of recreational tennis in my college years. I loved being outside and enjoyed the diversion from study and music practice. I especially liked to serve hard, relishing those aces flying off my racket. I even enjoyed chasing the ball around the court when the competition's skills were more advanced and refined than mine.

Even though I played simply for fun, I had an inner drive to get better. Playing against superior competition always coaxed that out. I would watch their footwork, racket angle, and court positioning, and then attempt to emulate what I saw. I couldn't be lazy and then expect to be in the game - a good thing!

Deciding on "stepping up my game," I took a tennis

lesson.

One.

Having played for years with many bad/lazy habits, I found the experience to be incredibly frustrating…and a little bit wonderful.

My coach went to work on my lazy footwork, my inconsistent service toss, my sloppy backhand, and various other fundamentals. It was painful for the moment but proved increasingly exhilarating as I noticed my game slowly improving over the hour. To this day, I cannot step on the court without hearing him bark his immensely helpful instructions in my head.

Whatever the discipline, technique refinement and skill development, accompanied by accumulated repetition will always yield results.

Two questions:

First one - have you had any success as a songwriter? That is…have you written some decent, usable songs that were recorded or sung at your church or even around the world?

Second question - have you become lazy? That is…have you allowed your success to stunt your growth as a songwriter, limiting what you can offer to those who need to not only hear but sing more of your songs?

One way laziness often pops up for me is in my chord choices. I do remember back to when I was joyfully experimenting with new keys, and sounds, and forms, and instrumentations…but a little success may have crept in, and stunted my growth, even if only a little bit.

Can you relate?

Then do what I have attempted to do over the years.

Expand your chord vocabulary. Practice them. Become familiar with their varying colors and tonal nuances. Experiment with voicings and sequence, then see what happens.

Next, try them in an actual game (in your songs).

Repeat.

Another semi-related point straight ahead.

I've often remarked to budding musicians over the years:

"Don't mistakenly label that "noodling around" on

your instrument "practice." That is called "warming up."

Practice is working on something that you can't do, something that you are not yet proficient in, a new mode, a new lick, a new chord…

Learn.

Practice what you learn.

#30
ask yourself, "do i want to sing it?" then "do i want to sing it again?"

The key word in this tip is "I."

You could be thinking right now, "Wait a minute! I've been told that I need to avoid the "I" in worship. It's not about me after all. It's about God…" (Insert all other guilt trips you've been forced to travel on).

My contention is that true worship is in fact about the "I." It is about me. It is not intended to be overtly nor exclusively focused on me, but I am involved!

My understanding of biblical worship is that it is an interaction, a relationship involving more than one party, in this case - A Holy God and me (a member of

WORSHIP SONGWRITING TIPS   david j. pedde

His Bride, the Church).

He invites us, and we respond. Worship.

He makes it possible and we come. Worship.

Now that we are talking about this, may I ask - what is your story?

There is something captivatingly authentic about listening in as a singer-songwriter narrates their own story set to music. A story always draws in the listener, particularly a true one.

I've often quoted the late Oscar Hammerstein who remarked,

> "Technique and professional polish do not make a song. There is an element much less tangible: sincerity." He pointed out that "most bad writing is the result of ignoring one's own experiences and contriving spurious emotions for spurious characters."[1]

Reading that quote the first time, I had to look up the word *spurious*.

It means "lacking authenticity or validity in essence or origin."[2]

So, here is the million dollar question: Are your songs authentic and valid, arising naturally out of your love relationship with Jesus Christ? Are they songs that you can simply not stop singing?

It is awe-inspiring for me to reflect now and then on the poignant words of Zephaniah 3:17 (look it up!). When I meditate on the fact that He "rejoices over me (me!) with singing,"[3] I cannot contain my bursting heart nor my rising song of worship to Him.

Is that your story?

Sing then.

Sing in response to all that God has done for you in Christ.

Allow the Holy Spirit, Who dwells inside of you, to inspire your song to Him.

Join the chorus of heaven with a "Holy, Holy, Holy."

This is your story. This is your song.

AFTERWORD

I wrote my first worship song in the late 1970's as a result of a new found love relationship with Christ. I was exceedingly grateful to Him for His mercy, His grace, and His unconditional love. I wrote about it, sang about it, and led others in that song ("Child of the King"), along with many others.

I wrote in earnest and volume throughout the 1980's, developed my craft through trial and error, and was privileged to lead those songs at my church and around the world.

I taught my first songwriting class in the 1990's and now have continued mentoring songwriters ever since. As mentioned in the foreword of this book, that's forty years, give or take.

Do you have a life verse, a passage of scripture that God has "stamped" over your life?

Here's mine:

> I waited patiently for the Lord;
> And He inclined to me and heard my cry.
> He brought me up out of the pit of
> destruction, out of the miry clay,
> And He set my feet upon a rock making my
> footsteps firm.
> He put a new song in my mouth, a song of
> praise to our God;
> Many will see and fear
> And will trust in the Lord.[1]
>   Psalm 40:1-3 NASB

I vividly remember reading those words for the first time in 1979 and understanding that they were for me! It became providential for me to write and sing those songs of praise to God, then to watch Him fulfill His promises regarding the "many."

Since then, my song output has gone up and down, but by His grace and enabling, I have remained faithful to that calling.

I suspect that you read this book because of a similar calling on your life.

So, go for it.

Sing that new song, and write it down, and lead it, and

record it for others to be able to join in the song as they see, fear and trust in the Lord.

Lastly, I'd love to hear from you. I'd love to hear your songs. I'd love to have a part in sharing them with others.

Blessings,

Dave

NOTES

#2 study form

1. Sheila Davis, *The Craft of Lyric Writing* (Cincinnati, OH: Writer's Digest Books, 1985), 25.

2. Two separate references to the study of fences can be seen in the following articles:

Terrence Seamon, *On the Value of Fences.* http://hr.blognotions.com/2012/03/01/on-the-value-of-fences/ First accessed October 17, 2016, 8:00 A.M.

Will Krieger, *Lessons from the Playground,* http://repassinc.com/2016/04/4125/ First accessed October 17, 2016, 8:12 A.M.

#4 write often

1. Don Wyrtzen, *A Musician Looks at the Psalms: 365 Daily Meditations* (Nashville, TN: Broadman & Holman Publishers, 2004), 80.

#5 pray often

1. "…God is love. We know how much God loves us, and we have put our trust in His love. God is love, and all who live in love live in God, and God lives in them." I John 4:8b, 16 NLT.

2. Andy Park, *To Know You More: Cultivating the Heart of the Worship Leader* (Downers Grove, IL: InterVarsity Press, 2002).

#6 write a call to worship

1. Taken from my lecture: *The Worship Leader's Job Description. Worship First Principles: A brief look at the essentials for Christian Worship.*

#7 read a psalm

1. https://www.biblegateway.com/versions/ Message-MSG-Bible/ First accessed October 10, 2016, 9:00 A.M.
2. Ibid.
3. David J. Pedde, *The Planting: Make Me New / Make in Me a Clean Heart ©2000* MAKERmusicMakers
4. http://www.christianitytoday.com/history/ people/poets/isaac-watts.html First accessed November 10, 2016, 9:17 A.M.

#13 write a bumper

1. David J. Pedde, *Before the Stars: My Best Friend ©1986, 1999* MAKERmusicMakers

#17 write one hook per day

1. http://www.goodreads.com/author/ quotes/102079 First accessed December 17, 2016, 4:47 P.M.

#18 ask if a pre-chorus is necessary

1. Sheila Davis, *The Craft of Lyric Writing* (Cincinnati, OH: Writer's Digest Books, 1985), 63.
2. Ibid.

#19 try avoiding certain words

1. http://www.epiclesis.org/podcasts/60-seconds-with-robert-e-webber/ First accessed January 17, 2017, 8:01 A.M.
2. https://iws.edu/2016/10/oct-31-2016-its-all-about-me/ First accessed January 17, 2017, 8:03 A.M.

#20 use one idea

1. https://www.forbes.com/sites/kevinkruse/ 2012/07/16/the-7-habits/#4b843bc639c6 First accessed January 10, 2017, 10:00 A.M.

#21 write a prayer
1. David J. Pedde, *Prayer Primer: Morning or Evening Prayers* (Milton, ON: MAKERmusicMakers, 2016).
2. Luke 22:42 NKJV
3. David J. Pedde, *The Planting: Come Now, Your Kingdom ©1996* MAKERmusicMakers

#24 acquire thesis input
1. https://www.goodreads.com/quotes/   178425-the-single-biggest-problem-in-communication-is-the-illusion-that First accessed January 24, 2017, 11:00 A.M.

#25 sing your prayers
1. David J. Pedde, *The Planting: I Believe ©2002* MAKERmusicMakers
2. Mark 9:24b

#27 whistle it
1. David J. Pedde, *Lord, Be Glorified (In the Life of Your Servant) ©1985 MAKERmusicMakers*
2. Bob Kilpatrick, *Lord, Be Glorified ©1978 Bob Kilpatrick Ministries*

#30 sing it again
1. Sheila Davis, *The Craft of Lyric Writing* (Cincinnati, OH: Writer's Digest Books, 1985), 264.
2. http://www.thefreedictionary.com/spurious First Accessed October 12, 2016 4:14 P.M.
3. Zephaniah 3:17

Afterword
1. Psalm 40:1-3

ABOUT THE AUTHOR

david.j.pedde | your.worship.mentor

worship leader | songwriter | producer | educator | coach | consultant | author

...helping worship leaders and pastors rethink what they do and redo what they think...

Dave has been involved in worship ministries for 40 years, although he doesn't really want anyone to believe he is that old. Originally from Edmonton, Alberta, he has served as worship pastor in 7 churches in

Canada and the U.S. and worked as Composer in Residence at North Central University in Minneapolis for 18 years where worship and songwriting were among his academic specialties.

He frequently travels as featured speaker, worship leader, teacher, and coach, and has extensive studio experience having produced 32 or so albums to date. Dave has over 100 published songs, with his most recent recordings being Windows Volume One and The Planting.

Dave earned his Masters degree from The Robert E. Webber Institute for Worship Studies and has served as Founder and President of Sanctus School for Worshippers.

Dave and Debbie have been married 36 years and have five children. He likes coffee, baseball and mornings...

Made in the USA
Columbia, SC
22 February 2019